The ESSENTIALS of

United States History

1789–1841
The Developing Nation

John F. Chilton, Ph.D.
Chair, Department of History and Social Sciences
Trevecca Nazarene College
Nashville, TN

Research & Education Association
Visit our website at
www.rea.com

Research & Education Association
61 Ethel Road West
Piscataway, New Jersey 08854
E-mail: info@rea.com

THE ESSENTIALS®
OF UNITED STATES HISTORY
1789 to 1841
The Developing Nation

Published 2009

Printed in the United States of America

Library of Congress Control Number 98-68662

ISBN-13: 978-0-87891-713-6
ISBN-10: 0-87891-713-6

What REA's Essentials® of History Will Do for You

REA's *Essentials® of History* offer an approach to the study of history that is a marked departure from what has been available traditionally. Our books are designed to steer a sensible middle course by including neither too much nor too little information.

For students, our books will help you with studying, getting through homework, writing papers, and preparing for exams. In these pocket volumes you'll find the important events and notable figures that shaped history, and the context in which to consider them.

For instructors, these books can assist in reviewing or modifying course outlines. They also provide excellent material for exams and writing assignments.

REA's authors are respected experts in their fields. They present clear, well-reasoned explanations and interpretations of the complex political, social, cultural, economic, and philosophical issues and developments that characterize each era.

In preparing the *Essentials® of History,* REA has made every effort to ensure their accuracy and maximize their usefulness. We believe you will find this series enjoyable and informative.

Larry B. Kling
Program Director

About the Author

John F. Chilton holds numerous graduate-level degrees in social science education, American history, economics, psychology, and accounting; and is a specialist in the early history of the United States.

Among his professional memberships are the Organization of American Historians, the Southern Historical Society, the Tennessee Historical Society, the Georgia Historical Society, Phi Delta Kappa, the Society for History Education, and the National Council for the Social Studies. He has published numerous articles on the Holiness Movement, and is currently chairman of the Department of History and Social Science at Trevecca Nazarene College in Nashville, Tennessee.

CONTENTS

CHAPTER 1

THE FEDERALIST ERA

The results of the first elections held under the new Constitution made it clear that the fledgling government was going to be managed by those who had drawn up the document and by their supporters. Few Antifederalists were elected to Congress, and many of the new legislators had served as delegates to the Philadelphia Convention two years before. This Federalist majority immediately set about to draft legislation which would fill in the gaps left by the convention and to erect the structure of a strong central government.

1.1 THE NEW EXECUTIVE

There had never been any doubt as to who would be the first President. George Washington received virtually all the votes of the presidential electors, and John Adams received the next highest number, thus becoming the Vice President. After a triumphal journey from Mount Vernon, Washington was inaugurated in New York City, the temporary seat of government, on April 30, 1789.

1.2 CONGRESS ERECTS THE STRUCTURE OF GOVERNMENT

The new national legislature immediately acted to honor the Federalist pledge of a bill of rights made to those voters who had hesitated to ratify the new Constitution. Twelve amendments were drafted which embodied the guarantees of personal liberties, most of which had been traditionally enjoyed by English citizens. Ten of these were ratified by the states by the end of 1791, and they became our Bill of Rights. The first nine spelled out specific guarantees of personal freedoms, such as religion, speech, press, assembly, petition, and a speedy trial by one's peers, and the Tenth Amendment reserved to the states all those powers not specifically withheld, or granted to the federal government. This last was a concession to those who feared the potential of the central government to usurp the sovereignty of the individual states.

1.3 THE ESTABLISHMENT OF THE FEDERAL COURT SYSTEM

The Judiciary Act of 1789 provided for a Supreme Court, with six justices, and invested it with the power to rule on the constitutional validity of state laws. It was to be the interpreter of the "supreme law of the land." A system of district courts was established to serve as courts of original jurisdiction, and three courts of appeal were also provided for.

1.4 THE ESTABLISHMENT OF THE EXECUTIVE DEPARTMENTS

The Constitution had not specified the names or number of the departments of the executive branch. Congress established three — state, treasury, and war — and also the offices of attorney-general and postmaster-general. President Washington immediately appointed Thomas Jefferson, Alexander Hamilton, and Henry Knox, respectively, to fill the executive posts, and Edmund Randolph became attorney general. These four men were called upon regularly by the president for advice, and they later formed the nucleus of what became known as the Cabinet, although no provision for such was made in the Constitution.

1.5 WASHINGTON'S ADMINISTRATION, 1789 – 1797

1.5.1 Hamilton's Financial Program

Treasury Secretary Alexander Hamilton, in his "Report on the Public Credit," proposed the funding of the national debt at face value, federal assumption of state debts, and the establishment of a national bank. In his "Report on Manufactures," Hamilton proposed an extensive program for federal stimulation of industrial development, through subsidies and tax incentives. The money needed to fund these programs, proposed Hamilton, would come from an excise tax on distillers and from tariffs on imports.

1.5.2 Opposition to Hamilton's Program

Jefferson and others objected to the funding proposal because it obviously would benefit speculators who had bought up state and confederation obligations at depressed prices, and now would profit handsomely by their redemption at face value. The original purchasers, they claimed, should at least share in the windfall. They opposed the tax program because it would fall primarily on the small farmers. They saw

Hamilton's entire program as enriching a small elite group at the expense of the more worthy common citizen.

1.5.3 The Appearance of Political Parties

Political parties had been considered a detrimental force by the founding fathers, since they were seen to contribute to the rise of "factions." Thus no mention of such was made in the Constitution. But differences in philosophy very quickly began to drive the leaders of government into opposing camps — the Federalists and the Republicans.

Alexander Hamilton and the Federalists. Hamilton, as the theorist of the group who favored a strong central government, interpreted the Constitution as having vested extensive powers in the federal government. This "implied powers" stance claimed that the government was given all powers that were not expressly denied to it. This is the "broad" interpretation.

Thomas Jefferson and the Republicans. Jefferson and Madison held the view that any action not specifically permitted in the Constitution was thereby prohibited. This is the "strict" interpretation, and the Republicans opposed the establishment of Hamilton's national bank on this view of government. The Jeffersonian supporters, primarily under the guidance of James Madison, began to organize political groups in opposition to the Federalist program, and called themselves Republicans.

Sources of Partisan Support. The Federalists received their strongest support from the business and financial groups in the commercial centers of the Northeast and in the port cities of the South. The strength of the Republicans lay primarily in the rural and frontier areas of the South and West.

1.5.4 Foreign Affairs

The French Revolution. When revolutionary France went to war with the European powers in 1792, Washington's response was a *Proclamation of Neutrality.* Citizen Genet violated that policy by trying to encourage popular support in this country for the French government, and embarrassed the president. American merchants traded with both sides, though the most lucrative business was carried on with the French West Indies. This brought retaliation by the British, who began to seize American merchant ships and force their crews into service with the British navy.

Jay's Treaty with Britain (1794). John Jay negotiated a treaty with the British which attempted to settle the conflict at sea, as well as to curtail English agitation of their Indian allies on the western borders. The agreement actually settled few of the issues and merely bought time for the new nation in the worsening international conflict. Jay was severely criticized for his efforts, and was even hanged in effigy, but the Senate accepted the treaty as the best possible under the circumstances.

The Treaty with Spain (1795). Thomas Pinckney was invited to the Spanish court to strengthen what Madrid perceived to be her deteriorating position on the American frontier. The result was the *Pinckney Treaty*, ratified by the Senate in 1796, in which the Spanish opened the Mississippi River to American traffic, including the right of deposit in the port city of New Orleans, and recognized the 31st parallel as the northern boundary of Florida.

1.5.5 Frontier Problems

Indian tribes on the Northwest and Southwest borders were increasingly resisting the encroachments on their lands by the

American settlers. British authorities in Canada were encouraging the Indians in their depredations against frontier settlements.

In 1794, General Anthony Wayne decisively defeated the Indians at the Battle of Fallen Timbers, and the resulting *Treaty of Greenville* cleared the Ohio territory of Indian tribes.

1.5.6 Internal Problems

The Whiskey Rebellion **(1794).** Western farmers refused to pay the excise tax on whiskey which formed the backbone of Hamilton's revenue program. When a group of Pennsylvania farmers terrorized the tax collectors President Washington sent out a federalized militia force of some 15,000 men, and the rebellion evaporated, thus strengthening the credibility of the young government.

Land Policy. As the original 13 states ceded their Western land claims to the new federal government, new states were organized and admitted to the Union, thus strengthening the ties of the Western farmers to the central government (Vermont, 1791; Kentucky, 1792; and Tennessee, 1796).

1.6 JOHN ADAMS' ADMINISTRATION, 1797 – 1801

1.6.1 The Election of 1796

John Adams was the Federalist candidate, and Thomas Jefferson ran under the opposition banner of the Republicans. Since Jefferson received the second highest number of electoral votes, he became Vice-President. Thus, a Federalist president and a Republican vice-president served together, an obviously awkward arrangement. Adams was a brilliant lawyer and statesman, but too dogmatic and uncompromising to be an effective politician, and he endured a very frustrating and unproductive term in office.

1.6.2   Troubles with France

The XYZ Affair. A three-man delegation was sent to France in 1798 to persuade the French to stop harassing American shipping. When they were solicited for a bribe by three subordinates of the French Minister Talleyrand, they indignantly refused, and their report of this insult produced outrage at home. The cry "millions for defense, but not one cent for tribute" was raised, and public feelings against the French ran high. Since Talleyrand's officials were unnamed in the dispatches, the incident became known as the "XYZ Affair."

Quasi-War, 1798 – 1799. This uproar moved Adams to suspend all trade with the French, and American ship captains were authorized to attack and capture armed French vessels. Congress created a Department of the Navy, and war seemed imminent. In 1800, the new French government, now under Napoleon, signed a new treaty, and the peace was restored.

1.6.3   Repression and Protest

The Alien and Sedition Acts. The elections in 1798 had increased the Federalist majorities in both houses of Congress and they used their "mandate" to enact legislation to stifle foreign influences. The *Alien Act* raised new hurdles in the path of immigrants trying to obtain citizenship, and the *Sedition Act* widened the powers of the Adams administration to muzzle its newspaper critics. Both bills were aimed at actual or potential Republican opposition, and a number of editors were

7

actually jailed for printing critical editorials.

The Kentucky and Virginia Resolves. Republican leaders were convinced that the Alien and Sedition Acts were unconstitutional but the process of deciding on the constitutionality of federal laws was as yet undefined. Jefferson and Madison decided that the state legislatures should have that power, and they drew up a series of resolutions which were presented to the Kentucky and Virginia legislatures, respectively. They proposed that John Locke's "compact theory" be applied, which would empower the state bodies to "nullify" federal laws within those states. These resolutions were adopted, but only in those two states, and so the issue died, but a principle was put forward which was later to bear fruit in the nullification controversy of the 1830's and finally in the secession crisis of 1860 – 61.

1.7   THE REVOLUTION OF 1800

1.7.1   *The Election*

Thomas Jefferson and Aaron Burr ran on the Republican ticket, against John Adams and Charles Pinckney for the Federalists. The Republican candidates won handily, but both received the same number of electoral votes, thus throwing the selection of the President into the House of Representatives. After a lengthy deadlock, Alexander Hamilton threw his support to Jefferson, and Burr had to accept the Vice-Presidency, the result obviously intended by the electorate. This increased the ill-will between Hamilton and Burr and contributed to their famous duel in 1804.

1.7.2 Packing the Judiciary

The Federalist Congress passed a new Judiciary Act early in 1801 and President Adams filled the newly created vacancies with party supporters, many of them with last-minute commissions. John Marshall was then appointed Chief Justice of the U.S. Supreme Court, thus guaranteeing continuation of Federalist policies from the bench of the high court.

CHAPTER 2

THE JEFFERSONIAN ERA

Thomas Jefferson and his Republican followers envisioned a society in vivid contrast to that of Hamilton and the Federalists. They dreamed of a nation of independent farmers, living under a central government that exercised a minimum of control over their lives and served merely to protect the individual liberties guaranteed by the Constitution. This agrarian paradise would be free from the industrial smoke and urban blight of Europe, and would serve as a beacon light of Enlightenment rationalism to a world searching for direction. That vision was to prove a mirage, and Jefferson was to preside over a nation that was growing more industrialized and urban, and which seemed to need an ever stronger hand at the presidential tiller.

2.1 THE NEW FEDERAL CITY

The city of Washington had been designed by Pierre L'Enfant and was briefly occupied by the Adams administration. When Jefferson moved in, it was still a straggling provincial town, with muddy streets and muggy summers. Most of its inhabitants moved out when Congress was not in session.

2.2 JEFFERSON THE PRESIDENT

The new president tried to project an image of democratic simplicity, sometimes appearing so casually dressed as to appear slovenly. But he was a brilliant thinker and a shrewd politician. He appointed men to his cabinet who agreed with his political philosophy: James Madison as Secretary of State and Albert Gallatin to the Treasury.

2.2.1 Conflict with the Judges

Marbury vs. Madison. William Marbury, one of Adams' "midnight appointments," sued Secretary of State Madison to force delivery of his commission as a justice of the peace in the federal district. John Marshall, as Supreme Court justice, refused to rule on the request, claiming that the law which gave the Supreme Court jurisdiction over such matters had exceeded the Constitutional grant of powers and thus was unconstitutional. Marshall thus asserted the power of judicial review over federal legislation, a power which has become the foundation of the Supreme Court's check on the other two branches of government.

The Impeachment Episodes. Jefferson began a campaign to remove Federalist judges by impeachment. One district judge was removed, and proceedings were begun to impeach Supreme Court Justice Samuel Chase. That effort failed, but the threat had encouraged the judiciary to be less blatantly political.

11

2.2.2 Domestic Affairs

Enforcement of the Alien and Sedition Acts was immediately suspended, and the men convicted under those laws were released.

The federal bureaucracy was reduced and expenses were drastically cut. The size of the army was reduced and the expansion program of the navy was cancelled.

The excise taxes were repealed and federal income was limited to land sale proceeds and customs duties. Federal land sale policy was liberalized, smaller parcels were authorized, and less cash was required – policies which benefitted small farmers.

The Twelfth Amendment was adopted and ratified in 1804, ensuring that a tie vote between candidates of the same party could not again cause the confusion of the Jefferson-Burr affair.

Following the Constitutional mandate, the importation of slaves was stopped by law in 1808.

2.2.3 The Louisiana Purchase

The International Scene. Napoleon, in an effort to regain some of France's New World empire, had obtained the old French trans-Mississippi territory from Spain by political pressure. Jefferson sent a delegation to Paris to try to buy New Orleans, lest the new French officials close it to American traffic. Napoleon's defeat in Santo Domingo persuaded him that Louisiana could not be exploited, and indeed was now subject to potential American incursions. So he offered to sell the entire territory to the United States for $15 million. The Ameri-

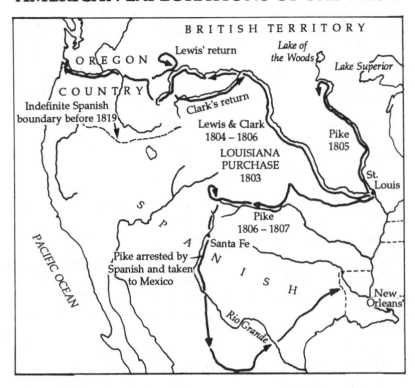

can delegation accepted the offer in April, 1803, even though they had no authority to buy more than the city of New Orleans.

The Constitutional Dilemma. Jefferson's stand on the strict interpretation of the Constitution would not permit him to purchase land without Congressional approval. But he accepted his advisors' counsel that his treaty-making powers included the authority to buy the land. Congress concurred, after the fact, and the purchase price was appropriated, thus doubling the territory of the nation overnight.

Exploring the West. Even before Napoleon's offer, Jefferson had authorized an expedition to explore the Western territory to the Pacific. The Lewis and Clark group, with 48 men, left St. Louis in 1804, and returned two years later with a wealth of scientific and anthropological information, and having strengthened the United States' claim to the Oregon territory. At the same time, Zebulon Pike and others had been traversing the middle parts of Louisiana and mapping the land.

2.2.4 Problems at Home

The Essex Junto (1804). Some New England Federalists saw the Western expansion as a threat to their position in the Union, and they tried to organize a secessionist movement. They courted Aaron Burr's support by offering to back him in a bid for the governorship of New York. Hamilton led the opposition to that campaign and when Burr lost the election, he challenged Hamilton to a duel, which resulted in Hamilton's death.

The Burr Conspiracy. Aaron Burr was now a fugitive, without a political future. He became involved in a scheme to take Mexico from Spain and establish a new nation in the West.

In the fall of 1806, he led a group of armed men down the Mississippi River system toward New Orleans. He was arrested in Natchez and tried for treason in Richmond, Virginia. Judge John Marshall's decision for acquittal helped to narrow the legal definition of treason.

Jefferson's attempts to influence and prejudice the trial were justified by his claims of "executive privilege," but they were fruitless.

14

John Randolph and the Yazoo Claims. Jefferson's Republican opponents, under the leadership of his cousin John Randolph of Roanoke, called themselves the "Quids." They accused the president of complicity in the Yazoo Land controversy which had followed Georgia's cession of her western lands to the federal government. This created serious strife within the Republican party and weakened Jefferson's effectiveness in his second term.

2.3 INTERNATIONAL INVOLVEMENT

2.3.1 *The Barbary War*

In 1801 Jefferson sent a naval force to the Mediterranean to break the practice of the North African Muslim rulers of exacting tribute from Western merchant ships. Intermittent undeclared war dragged on until 1805, with no decisive settlement.

2.3.2 *The Napoleonic Wars*

War continued in Europe between France under Napoleon and the European powers led by Britain. Both sides tried to prevent trade with their enemies by neutral powers, especially the United States. Napoleon's "Continental System" was answered by Britain's "Orders in Council." American ships were seized by both sides and American sailors were "impressed" into the British navy.

2.3.3 *The* Chesapeake-Leopard *Affair* (1807)

The British ship H.M.S. *Leopard* stopped the U.S.S. *Chesapeake* off the Chesapeake Bay, and four alleged British deserters were taken off. Public outcry for war followed, and Jefferson was hard pressed to remain neutral.

2.3.4 *The Embargo of 1807*

Jefferson's response to the cry for war was to draft a law prohibiting American ships from leaving port for any foreign destination, thus avoiding contact with vessels of either belligerent. The result was economic depression, particularly in the heavily commercial Northeast. This proved to be his most unpopular policy of both terms in office.

2.4 MADISON'S ADMINISTRATION, 1809 – 1817

2.4.1 *The Election of 1808*

Republican James Madison won the election over Federalist Charles Pinckney, but the Federalists gained seats in both houses of the Congress. The embargo-induced depression was obviously a heavy political liability, and Madison was to face growing pressures to deal with the international crisis. He was a brilliant man but with few social or political skills. His greatest asset was probably his wife, the vivacious and energetic Dolly.

2.4.2 *The War of 1812*

Background. Congress had passed a modified embargo just before Madison's inauguration, known as the Non-Intercourse Act, which opened trade to all nations except France and Britain. When it expired in 1810, it was replaced by Macon's Bill No. 2, which gave the president power to prohibit trade with any nation when they violated U.S. neutrality.

The Indian tribes of the Northwest and the Mississippi Valley were resentful of the government's policy of pressured removal to the West, and the British authorities in Canada were exploiting their discontent by encouraging border raids against the American settlements.

The Shawnee chief Tecumseh set out to unite the Mississippi Valley tribes and re-establish Indian dominance in the Old Northwest. With the help of his brother, the Prophet, and the timely New Madrid earthquake, he persuaded a sizeable force of warriors to join him. On November 11, 1811, General William Henry Harrison destroyed Tecumseh's village on Tippecanoe Creek and dashed his hopes for an Indian confederacy.

Southern frontiersmen coveted Spanish Florida, which included the southern ranges of Alabama, Mississippi and Louisiana. They resented Spanish support of Indian depredations against the borderlands, and since Spain was Britain's ally, they saw Britain as the background cause of their problems.

The Congress in 1811 contained a strong pro-war group called the War Hawks, led by Henry Clay and John C. Calhoun. They gained control of both houses and began agitating for war with the British. On June 1, 1812, President Madison asked for a declaration of war, and Congress complied.

2.4.3   The War in the North

A three-pronged invasion of Canada met with disaster on all three fronts, and the Americans fell back to their own borders. At sea, American privateers and frigates, including "Old Ironsides," scored early victories over British warships, but were soon driven back into their home ports and blockaded by the powerful British ships-of-the-line.

Admiral Oliver Hazard Perry constructed a fleet of ships on Lake Erie and on September 10, 1813, defeated a British force

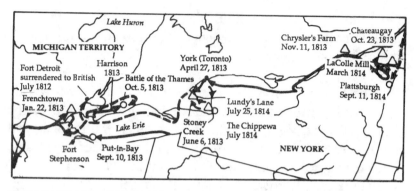

THE WAR OF 1812

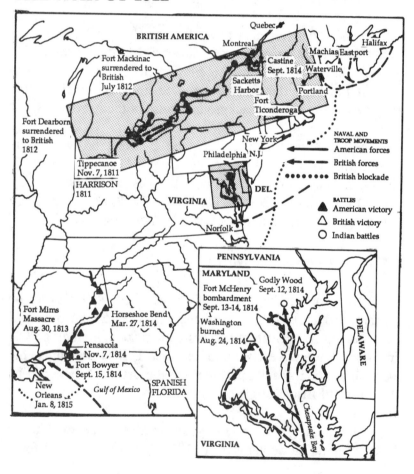

at Put-In Bay and established control of the lake. His flagship flew the banner, "Don't Give Up the Ship." This victory opened the way for William Henry Harrison to invade Canada in October and defeat a combination British and Indian force at the Battle of the Thames.

2.4.4 The War in the Southwest

Andrew Jackson led a force of frontier militia into Alabama in pursuit of Creek Indians who had massacred the white inhabitants of Fort Mims. On March 27, 1814, he crushed the Indians at Horseshoe Bend, and then seized the Spanish garrison at Pensacola.

2.4.5 British Strategy Changes, 1814

Invasion from Canada. A British force came down Lake Champlain and met defeat at Plattsburgh, New York in September.

Invasion of the Chesapeake Bay. A British armada sailed up the Bay and sacked and burned Washington, D.C. They then proceeded up the Bay toward Baltimore, which was guarded by Fort McHenry. That fort held firm through the British bombardment, inspiring Key's "Star Spangled Banner."

The Battle of New Orleans. The most serious British threat came at the port of New Orleans. A powerful invasion force was sent there to close the mouth of the Mississippi River, but Andrew Jackson decisively defeated it with a polyglot army of frontiersmen, blacks, creoles and pirates. The battle was fought on January 8, 1815, two weeks after a peace treaty had been signed at the city of Ghent, in Belgium.

19

2.4.6 The Treaty of Ghent, Christmas Eve 1814

With the European wars ended, the major causes for the dispute with Britain had ceased to be important, so both sides were eager for peace. The treaty provided for the acceptance of the status quo at the beginning of hostilities and so both sides restored their wartime conquests to the other.

2.4.7 The Hartford Convention, December 1814

The Federalists had become increasingly a minority party. They vehemently opposed the war and Daniel Webster and other New England Congressmen consistently blocked the Administration's efforts to prosecute the war effort. On December 15, 1814, delegates from the New England states met in Hartford, Connecticut, and drafted a set of resolutions suggesting nullification – and even secession – if their interests were not protected against the growing influence of the South and the West.

Soon after the convention adjourned the news of the victory at New Orleans was announced and their actions were discredited. The Federalist party ceased to be a political force from this point.

2.4.8 Post-War Developments

Protective Tariff (1816). The first protective tariff in the nation's history was passed in 1816 to slow the flood of cheap British manufactures into the country.

Rush-Bagot Treaty (1817). An agreement was reached in 1817 between Britain and the United States to stop maintaining armed fleets on the Great Lakes. This first "disarmament" agreement is still in effect.

Jackson's Florida Invasion (1817). Indian troubles in the newly acquired areas of western Florida prompted General Andrew Jackson, acting under dubious authority, to invade Spanish East Florida and to hang two British subjects whom he suspected of selling guns and supplies to the Indians. Then he re-occupied Pensacola and raised the American flag, a clear violation of international law. Only wide public support prevented his arrest and prosecution by the government.

Indian Policy. The government began to systematically pressure all the Indian tribes remaining in the East to cede their lands and accept new homes west of the Mississippi, a policy which met with disappointing results. Most declined the offer.

The Barbary Wars (1815). In response to continued piracy and extortion in the Mediterranean, Congress declared war on the Muslim state of Algiers in 1815, and dispatched a naval force to the area under Stephen Decatur. He quickly defeated the North African pirates and forced them to pay indemnities for past tribute they had exacted from American ship captains. This action finally gained the United States free access to the Mediterranean basin.

The Adams-Onis Treaty (1819). Spain had decided to sell the remainder of the Florida territory to the Americans before they took it anyway. Under this agreement, the Spanish surrendered all their claims to the territory and drew the boundary of Mexico all the way to the Pacific. The United States in exchange agreed to assume $5 million in debts owed to American merchants.

The Monroe Doctrine. Around 1810, national revolutions had begun in Latin America, so the colonial populations refused to accept the rule of the new Napoleonic governments in Europe. Leaders like San Martin and Bolivar had declared in-

BOUNDARIES ESTABLISHED
BY TREATIES

BRITISH CANADA

54°40'

OREGON
COUNTRY
(Joint occupation
Great Britain and US, 1818;
ceded by Spain, 1819)

······· British Treaty line 1818

MICHIGAN
TERRITORY
(1818-1834)

UNORGANIZED
TERRITORY
1821

Adams – Onis Treaty line 1819

MEXICO
(Independent 1821)

Missouri

ARKANSAS
TERRITORY
1819-1824

PACIFIC OCEAN

SPANISH
TEXAS
1818-1836

Louisiana

······· Natural Boundary
of Lousiana country

Gulf of Mexico

dependence for their countries and, after Napoleon's fall in
1814, were defying the restored Hapsburg and Bourbon rulers
of Europe.

British and American leaders feared that the new European
governments would try to restore the former New World colo-

nies to their erstwhile royal owners.

In December 1823, President Monroe included in his annual message to Congress a statement that the American hemisphere was "henceforth not to be considered as subjects for future colonization by any European powers." Thus began a thirty-year period of freedom from serious foreign involvement for the United States.

CHAPTER 3

INTERNAL DEVELOPMENT, 1820 – 1830

The years following the War of 1812 were years of rapid economic and social development. Too rapid, in fact, and they were followed by a severe depression in 1819. But this slump was temporary, and it became obvious that the country was moving rapidly from its agrarian origins toward an industrial, urban future. Westward expansion accelerated, and the mood of the people became very positive. In fact, these years were referred to as the "Era of Good Feelings."

3.1   THE MONROE PRESIDENCY, 1817 – 1823

James Monroe, the last of the "Virginia Dynasty", had been hand-picked by the retiring Madison and he was elected with only one electoral vote opposed: a symbol of national unity.

3.1.1 *Post-War Boom*

The years following the war were characterized by a high foreign demand for American cotton, grain and tobacco; commerce flourished. The 2nd National Bank, through its overly-liberal credit policies, proved to be an inflationary influence, and the price level rose rapidly.

3.1.2 *The Depression of 1819*

Inventories of British manufactured goods had built up during the war, and English merchants began to dump their products on the American market at cut-rate prices. American manufacturers suffered from this influx of imports. The U.S. Bank tried to slow the inflationary spiral by tightening credit, and a sharp business slump resulted.

This depression was most severe in the newly expanding West, partly because of its economic dependency, partly because of heavy speculation in Western lands.

3.2 THE MARSHALL COURT

John Marshall delivered the majority opinions in a number of critical decisions in these formative years, all of which served to strengthen the power of the federal government and restrict the powers of state governments.

3.2.1 *Marbury v. Madison* (1803)

This case established the precedent of the Supreme Court's power to rule on the constitutionality of federal laws.

3.2.2 Fletcher v. Peck (1810)

The Georgia legislature had issued extensive land grants in a shady deal with the Yazoo Land Company. A subsequent legislative session repealed that action because of the corruption that had attended the original grant. The Court decided that the original action by the Georgia Assembly had constituted a valid contract which could not be broken regardless of the corruption which had followed. This was the first time a state law was voided on the grounds that it violated a principle of the U.S. Constitution.

3.2.3 Dartmouth College v. Woodward (1819)

The quarrel between the president and the trustees of the New Hampshire college became a political issue when the Republicans backed the president and the Federalists supported the trustees. The president tried to change Dartmouth from a private to a public institution by having its charter revoked. The Court ruled that the charter, though issued by the king during colonial days, still constituted a contract, and thus could not be arbitrarily changed or revoked without the consent of both parties. The result of this decision was to severely limit the power of state governments to control the corporation, which was the emerging form of business organization.

3.2.4 McCulloch v. Maryland (1819)

The state of Maryland had tried to levy a tax on the Baltimore branch of the Bank of the United States, and so protect the competitive position of its own state banks. Marshall's ruling declared that no state has the right to control an agency of the federal government. Since "the power to tax is the power to destroy," such state action violated Congress' "implied powers" to establish and operate a national bank.

3.2.5 *Gibbons v. Ogden* (1824)

The State of New York had granted a monopoly to Ogden to operate a steamboat between New York and New Jersey. Gibbons obtained a Congressional permit to operate a steamboat line in the same waters. When Ogden sued to maintain his monopoly, the New York courts ruled in his favor. Gibbons' appeal went to the Supreme Court. John Marshall ruled that commerce included navigation, and that only Congress has the right to regulate commerce among states. Thus the state-granted monopoly was void.

3.3 THE MISSOURI COMPROMISE (1820)

The Missouri Territory, the first to be organized from the Louisiana Purchase, applied for statehood in 1819. Since the Senate membership was evenly divided between slave-holding and free states at that time, the admission of a new state was obviously going to give the voting advantage either to the North or to the South. Slavery was already well-established in the new territory, so the Southern states were confident in their advantage, until Representative Tallmadge of New York proposed an amendment to the bill which would prohibit slavery in Missouri.

The Southern outcry was immediate, and the ensuing debate grew hot. The Senate was dead-locked.

3.3.1 *Henry Clay's Compromise Solution*

As the debate dragged on, the northern territory of Massachusetts applied for admission as the state of Maine. This offered a way out of the dilemma, and House Speaker Clay formulated a package that both sides could accept. The two ad-

THE MISSOURI COMPROMISE

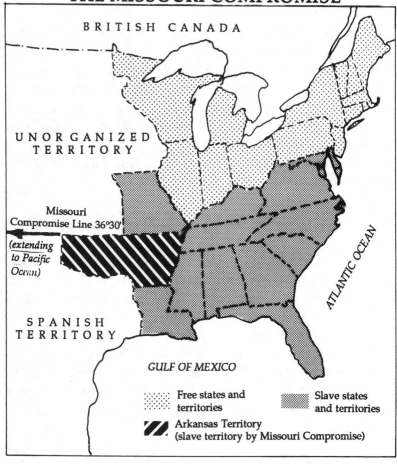

BRITISH CANADA

UNORGANIZED
TERRITORY

Missouri
Compromise Line 36°30'

*(extending
to Pacific
Ocean)*

SPANISH
TERRITORY

ATLANTIC OCEAN

GULF OF MEXICO

Free states and
territories

Slave states
and territories

Arkansas Territory
(slave territory by Missouri Compromise)

mission bills were combined, with Maine coming in free and
Missouri as a slave state. To make the package palatable for the
House, a provision was added to prohibit slavery in the remainder of the Louisiana Territory, north of the southern boundary
of Missouri (latitude 36 degrees 30'). Clay guided this bill
through the House and it became law, thus maintaining the
balance of power.

The debates in Congress had reminded everyone of the

deep division between the sections, and some saw it as evidence of trouble to come. Thomas Jefferson, in retirement at Monticello, remarked that the news from Washington was like a "fire-ball in the night."

3.4 THE EXPANDING ECONOMY

3.4.1 *The Growing Population*

Population continued to double every 25 years. The migration of people to the West increased in volume and by 1840 over one-third of all Americans lived west of the Alleghenies. Immigration from abroad was not significant until 1820; then it began to increase rapidly, mostly from the British Isles.

3.4.2 *The Farming Sector*

As markets for farm products grew in the expanding cities, coupled with liberal land sale policies by the federal government, the growing of staple agricultural crops became more profitable. More and more land was put into cultivation, and the prevailing system of clearing and planting became more wasteful of timber as well as of the fertility of the land.

3.4.3 *The Cotton Kingdom*

The new lands in the Southwest, then made up by Alabama, Mississippi, Louisiana and Texas, proved ideal for the production of short-staple cotton. Eli Whitney's invention of the cotton "gin" solved the problem of separating the seeds from the fibers, and the cotton boom was under way.

The growing market for food and work animals in the cotton South provided the opportunity for the new Western farmers to specialize in those items and further stimulated the westward movement.

3.4.4 Other Economic Developments

Fishing. New England and Chesapeake fishing proved very profitable. Deep-sea whaling became a significant enterprise, particularly from the Massachusetts/Rhode Island ports.

Lumbering. The expanding population created a need for building materials, and timber remained a profitable export item. Shipbuilding thrived in a number of Eastern Seaboard and Gulf Coast ports.

Fur Trade. John Jacob Astor and others opened up business all the way to the Northwest coast. "Mountain men" probed deeper and deeper into the Rocky Mountain ranges in search of the beaver.

Trade with the Spanish. The Santa Fe Trail, which ran from New Mexico northeast to Independence, Missouri, became an active trading corridor, opening up the Spanish territories to American migration and influence, and also providing the basis for future territorial claims.

3.5 THE TRANSPORTATION REVOLUTION

The first half of the 19th century witnessed an extraordinary sequence of inventions and innovations which produced a true revolution in transport and communications.

3.5.1   River Traffic

The steamboats built by Robert Fulton, the *Clermont* in 1807 and the *New Orleans* in 1811, transformed river transport. As shipment times and freight rates both plummeted, regular steam service was established on all the major river systems.

3.5.2   Roadbuilding

By 1818, the National Road, which was built with federal funds, had been completed from Cumberland, Maryland to Wheeling, Virginia, linking the Potomac with the Ohio River. A network of privately-owned toll roads (turnpikes) began to reach out from every sizeable city. They were usually built for only a few miles out, and they never accounted for a significant share of the total freight tonnage moved, but they formed the nucleus for a growing road system in the new nation.

3.5.3   The Canal Era

The Erie Canal, linking the Hudson River at Albany, New York, with Lake Erie, was completed in 1825 and became the first and most successful example. It was followed by a rash of construction until canals linked every major waterway system east of the Mississippi River.

Canals were the first development projects to receive large amounts of public funding. They ran east-west and so tied the new West to the old East, with later implications for sectional divisions.

3.5.4   The Rise of New York City

Its location as a transport hub, coupled with innovations in

31

CANALS IN THE NORTHEAST, 1860

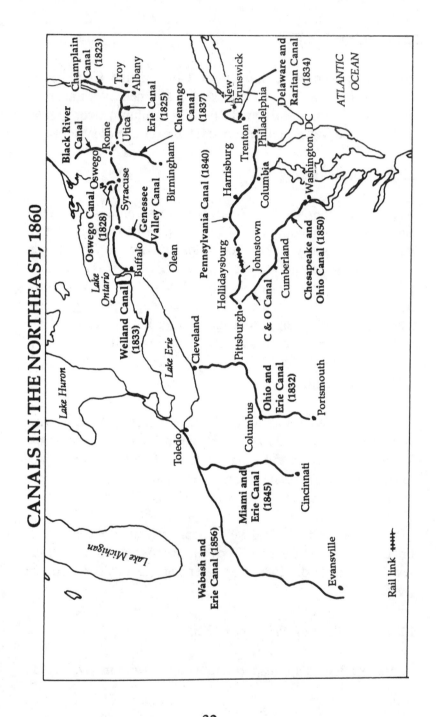

business practices, boosted New York City into a primary trade center, and America's largest city by 1830. One such innovation was the packet boat, which operated on a guaranteed schedule and helped to rationalize commerce, both internal and international.

New York soon dominated the domestic market for cotton, a situation which progressively reduced the South to the status of an economic colony.

3.6 INDUSTRIALIZATION

3.6.1 *The Rise of the Factory System*

Samuel Slater had migrated from Britain in 1789, having served as an apprentice under inventor Richard Arkwright and then as a mill manager. He used his knowledge to build the first successful cotton-spinning mill in this country. The first cotton manufacturing plant in the world to include all the elements of manufacturing under one roof was built in Boston in 1813.

Eli Whitney's development and application of the principle of interchangeable parts, first used in his firearms factories, helped to speed the growth of mass-production operations.

The expansion of markets in Latin America and the Far East, as well as domestic markets, both resulted from and helped to develop the factory system.

Manufacturers and industrialists found it necessary to organize banks, insurance companies, and real estate firms to meet the needs of their growing business organizations.

3.6.2 *The Corporation*

The corporate form, with its limited liability and its potential for raising and utilizing large amounts of capital, became the typical type of business organization. By the 1830's, most states had enacted general laws for incorporating.

3.6.3 *The Labor Supply*

In the early days, the "Lowell System" became a popular way to staff the New England factories. Young women were hired from the surrounding countryside, brought to town and housed in dormitories in the mill towns. They were paid low wages for hard work under poor conditions, but they were only working for a short time, to earn a dowry or help out with the family income, so they soon went back home. This "rotating labor supply" was ideal for the owners, since the girls were not motivated to agitate for better wages and conditions.

Labor was always in short supply in this country, so the system depended on technology to increase production. This situation always placed a premium on innovation in machinery and technique.

3.6.4 *The Growth of Unions*

The factory system separated the owners from the workers and thus depersonalized the workplace. It also made the skilled artisan less important, since the repetitive processes of the mill could be performed by relatively unskilled laborers.

Although the first organized strike took place in 1828, in Paterson, New Jersey, by child workers, periodic economic downturns helped keep workers relatively dependent and passive until the 1850's.

A major goal of early unions was the 10-hour day, and this effort sparked a period of growth in organized labor which was later effectively quenched by the depression of 1837.

3.7   EDUCATIONAL DEVELOPMENT

3.7.1   *The Growth of Public Schools*

Before 1815, there were no public schools to speak of in this country. Some states had endorsed the idea of free schools for the people, but they shrank from the task of financing such a system. Jefferson had outlined such a plan for Virginia, but it came to nothing.

Schools were primarily sponsored by private institutions — corporate academies in the Northeast and religious institutions in the South and mid-Atlantic states. Most were aristocratic in orientation, training the nation's leaders, and few had any interest in schooling the children of the poor.

Women were likewise considered unfit for academic training, and those female schools which existed concentrated on homemaking skills and the fine arts which would make "ornaments" of the young ladies enrolled.

The New York Free School, one of those rare examples of a school for the poor, experimented for a time with the Lancastrian system, in which older students tutored the younger ones, thus stretching the scarce budget dollars.

3.7.2   *Higher Education*

Although the numbers of institutions of higher learning increased sharply in the early years of the 19th century, none was truly public. All relied upon high tuition rates for survival, so less than one in ten young men, and no women, ever attended a college or university.

The training these schools provided was very limited as well. The only professional training was in theology, and only a scattering of colleges offered brief courses of study in law or medicine. The University of Pennsylvania, for example, offered one year of medical schooling, after which a person could obtain a license to practice the healing arts. Needless to say, medical practice was quite primitive.

3.8   THE GROWTH OF CULTURAL NATIONALISM

Jeffersonian Americans tried to demonstrate their newly-won independence by championing a strong sense of cultural nationalism, a feeling that their young republic represented the "final stage" of civilization, the "last great hope of mankind."

3.8.1   *Literary Nationalism*

Although most Americans had access to one or more newspapers, the market for native authors was quite limited. Publishers preferred to print works from British authors or to import books from Europe. A few Americans who were willing to pay the costs of publishing their own works found a growing number of readers.

3.8.2   *Significant American Authors*

Washington Irving was by far the best-known native writer in America. He excelled in the telling of folk tales and local color stories, and is best remembered for his portraits of

Hudson River characters.

Mercy Otis Warren, the revolutionary pamphleteer, published a multi-volume *History of the Revolution* in 1805.

"Parson" Mason Weems wrote the best-seller *Life of Washington* in 1806, which was short on historical accuracy but long on nationalistic hero-worship.

3.8.3 *Educational Literature*

Early schoolbooks, like Noah Webster's "Blue Backed Speller," as well as his dictionary of the "American" language, reflected the intense desire to promote patriotism and a feeling of national identity.

3.9 DEVELOPMENTS IN RELIGIOUS LIFE

3.9.1 *The Post-Revolution Years*

The Revolutionary War weakened the position of the traditional, established churches. The doctrines of the Enlightenment became very popular, and its religious expression, deism, gained a considerable following among the educated classes. Rationalism, Unitarianism, and Universalism all saw a period of popularity. Thomas Paine's exposition of the rationalist posture, *The Age of Reason*, attacked the traditional Christian values and was read widely.

3.9.2 *The Second Great Awakening*

The reaction to the trend toward rationalism, the decline in church membership, and the lack of piety, was a renewal of personal, heart-felt evangelicalism. It began in 1801 at Cane Ridge, Kentucky, in the first "camp meeting."

As the revival spread, its characteristics became more uniform — an emphasis on personal salvation, an emotional response to God's grace, an individualistic faith. Women took a major part in the movement. Blacks were also heavily involved, and the individualistic emphasis created unrest among their ranks, particularly in the slave-holding South.

The revival produced strong nationalistic overtones, and the Protestant ideas of a "called nation" were to flourish later in some of the Manifest Destiny doctrines of expansionism. The social overtones of this religious renewal were to spark the great reform movements of the 1830's and 1840's.

CHAPTER 4

THE JACKSONIAN DEMOCRACY, 1829-1841

While the "Age of Jackson" did not bring perfect political, social or economic equality to all Americans, it did mark a transformation in the political life of the nation that attracted the notice of European travelers and observers. Alexis de Tocqueville observed an "equality of condition" here that existed nowhere else in the world, and an egalitarian spirit among the people that was unique. Certainly the electorate had become broadened so that all white males had access to the polls, even if blacks and women were still outside the system. It was, in that sense, the "age of the common man." As to whether Andrew Jackson and his party were actually working for the good of those common men is another matter.

4.1 THE ELECTION OF 1824

4.1.1 *The Expansion of the Electorate*

Most states had already eliminated the property qualifications for voting before the campaigns for this election began.

The new Massachusetts state constitution of 1820 had led the way in this liberalization of the franchise, and most Northern states followed soon after, usually with some conservative opposition, but not violent reactions. In Rhode Island, Thomas Dorr led a bloodless "rebellion" in an effort to expand the franchise in that state, and though he was briefly imprisoned for his efforts, the incident led the conservative legislature to relent and grant the vote to non-property owners. The movement for reform was much slower in the Southern states.

Free blacks were excluded from the polls across the South, and in most of the Northern states. In those areas where they had held the franchise, they were gradually excluded from the social and economic mainstream as well as from the political arena in the early years of this period.

National elections had never attracted much enthusiasm until 1824. Legislative caucuses had made the presidential nominations and kept the ruling cliques in power by excluding the voters from the process. But this year the system failed, and the caucuses were bypassed.

The members of the electoral college were now being almost universally elected by the people, rather than by the state legislatures, as in the early days.

4.1.2 The Candidates

Secretary of the Treasury William H. Crawford of Georgia was the pick of the Congressional caucus.

Secretary of State John Quincy Adams held the job which traditionally had been the stepping-stone to the executive office.

Speaker of the House Henry Clay presented the only coherent program to the voters, the "American System," which provided a high tariff on imports to finance an extensive internal improvement package.

Andrew Jackson of Tennessee presented himself as a war hero from the 1812 conflict. All four candidates claimed to be Republicans.

4.1.3 The Election

Jackson won 43% of the popular vote, but the four-way split meant that he only received 38% of the electoral votes. Under the provisions of the 12th Amendment, the top three candidates were voted on by the House of Representatives. This left Henry Clay out of the running, and he threw his support to Adams. The votes had no sooner been counted, when the new president, Adams, appointed Henry Clay his Secretary of State.

Andrew Jackson and his supporters immediately cried "foul!" and accused Clay of making a deal for his vote. The rallying cry of "corrupt bargain" became the impetus for their immediate initiation of the campaign for the 1828 election.

4.2 THE ADAMS ADMINISTRATION

The new president pushed for an active federal government in areas like internal improvements and Indian affairs. These policies proved unpopular in an age of increasing sectional jealousies and conflicts over states' rights.

Adams was frustrated at every turn by his Jacksonian opposition, and his unwillingness, or inability, to compromise further antagonized his political enemies. For example, his refusal to endorse and enforce the Creek Indians' land cession to the state of Georgia was negated by their re-cession of their lands under pressure from Georgia's Jacksonian government.

4.3 JOHN C. CALHOUN AND NULLIFICATION

In 1828, Congress passed a new tariff bill which was originally supported by Southern Congressmen in order to embarrass the Administration. The finished bill, however, included higher import duties for many goods which were bought by Southern planters, so they bitterly denounced the law as the "Tariff of Abominations."

John C. Calhoun was serving as Adams' vice president, so to protest the tariff and still protect his position, he anonymously published the "South Carolina Exposition and Protest," which outlined his theory of the "concurrent majority": a Federal law which was deemed harmful to the interests of an individual state could be declared null and void within that state by a convention of the people. Thus, a state holding a minority position could ignore a law enacted by the majority which they considered unconstitutional (shades of Thomas Jefferson).

4.4 THE ELECTION OF 1828

Adams' supporters now called themselves the National Republicans, and Jackson's party ran as the Democratic Republicans. Andrew Jackson had aggressively campaigned since his defeat in the House in 1825.

It was a dirty campaign. Adams' people accused Jackson of adultery and of the murder of several militiamen who had been executed for desertion during the War of 1812. Jackson's followers in turn defamed Adams and his programs and accused him of extravagance with public funds.

When the votes were counted, Jackson had won 56% of the popular vote and swept 178 of the 261 electoral votes. John Calhoun was elected Vice President.

4.5 ANDREW JACKSON AS PRESIDENT

Jackson was popular with the common man. He seemed to be the prototype of the self-made Westerner: rough-hewn, violent, vindictive, with few ideas but strong convictions.

He ignored his appointed cabinet officers and relied instead on the counsel of his "Kitchen Cabinet," a group of partisan supporters who had the ear and the confidence of the president.

Jackson expressed the conviction that government operations could be performed by untrained, common folk, and he threatened the dismissal of large numbers of government employees, to replace them with his supporters. Actually, he talked more about this "spoils system" than he acted on it.

He exercised his veto power more than any other president before him. A famous example was the Maysville Road, a project in Kentucky which would require a Federal subsidy. Jackson opposed it because it would exist only within the boundaries of a single state.

4.6 JACKSONIAN INDIAN POLICY

Jackson supported the removal of all Indian tribes to west of the Mississippi River. The Indian Removal Act in 1830 provided for Federal enforcement of that process.

EXPULSION OF NATIVE AMERICANS FROM THE SOUTH, 1830 – 1835

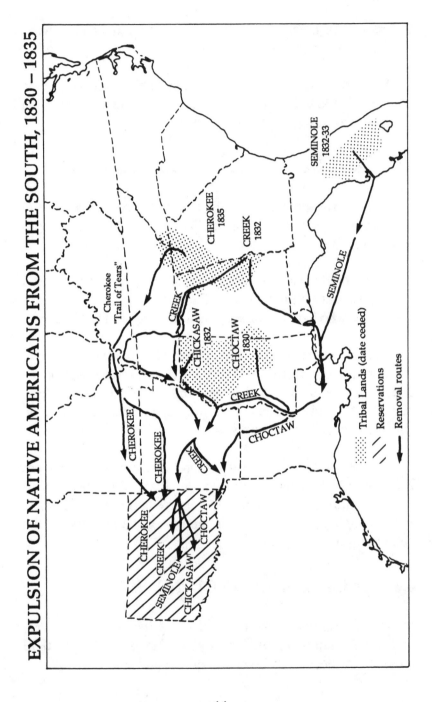

Cherokee "Trail of Tears"

CHEROKEE 1835

CREEK 1832

SEMINOLE 1832-33

SEMINOLE

CHICKASAW 1832

CHOCTAW 1830

CREEK

CHEROKEE

CHEROKEE

CREEK

CHOCTAW

CHEROKEE
CREEK
SEMINOLE
CHICKASAW
CHOCTAW

Tribal Lands (date ceded)

Reservations

Removal routes

The portion of the Cherokee Nation which occupied northern Georgia claimed to be a sovereign political entity within the boundaries of that state. The Supreme Court supported that claim in its decision in *Worcester vs. Georgia* (1832), but President Jackson refused to enforce the court's decision.

The result of this policy was the Trail of Tears, the forced march, under U.S. Army escort, of thousands of Cherokees to the West. A quarter or more of the Indians, mostly women and children, perished on the journey.

4.7   THE WEBSTER-HAYNE DEBATE (1830)

4.7.1   *Federal Land Policy*

The method of disposing of government land raised sectional differences. Westerners wanted cheap lands available to the masses. Northeasterners opposed this policy because it would lure away their labor supply and drive up wages. Southerners supported the West, hoping to weaken the ties between East and West.

4.7.2   *The Senate Confrontation*

Senator Robert Hayne of South Carolina made a speech in support of cheap land and he used Calhoun's anti-tariff arguments to support his position. In his remarks, he referred to the possibility of nullification.

Daniel Webster's famous replies to this argument moved the debate from the issue of land policy to the nature of the Union and states' rights within it. Webster argued for the Union as indissoluble and sovereign over the individual states. His concluding statements have become a part of our rhetorical heritage: "It is, Sir, the people's Constitution, the people's government, made for the people, made by the people, and answerable to the people. . . . Liberty and Union, now and for ever, one and inseparable!"

4.8   THE SECOND NULLIFICATION CRISIS

The final split between Andrew Jackson and his vice president, John C. Calhoun, came over the new Tariff of 1832, and over Mrs. Calhoun's snub of Peggy Eaton, the wife of Secretary of War John Eaton.

Mrs. Eaton was a commoner, and the aristocratic Mrs. Calhoun refused to include her on the guest lists for the Washington parties. Jackson, no doubt remembering the slights to his own dear Rachel, defended his friends Peggy and John, and demanded that they be included in the social life of the capitol.

Jackson was a defender of states' rights, but within the context of a dominant Union. When he supported the higher rates of the new tariff, Calhoun resigned his office in a huff and went home to South Carolina. There he composed an Ordinance of Nullification, which was duly approved by a special convention, and the customs officials were ordered to stop collecting the duties at the port of Charleston.

Jackson's response was immediate and decisive. He obtained a Force Bill from Congress (1833), which empowered him to use federal troops to enforce the collection of the taxes. And he suggested the possibility of hanging Calhoun. At the same time, he offered a gradual reduction in the levels of the duties. Calhoun backed down, both sides claimed victory, and the crisis was averted.

4.9   THE WAR ON THE BANK

4.9.1   *The Controversy*

The Bank of the United States had operated under the direction of Nicholas Biddle since 1823. He was a cautious man, and his conservative economic policy enforced conservatism among the state and private banks – which many bankers resented. Many of the Bank's enemies opposed it simply because it was big and powerful. Many still disputed its constitutionality.

4.9.2   *The Election of 1832*

Andrew Jackson freely voiced his antagonism toward the Bank and his intention to destroy it. During the campaign for the presidency in 1832, Henry Clay and Daniel Webster promoted a bill to recharter the Bank, even though its charter did not expire until 1836. They feared that Jackson would gain support over time and could kill the Bank as a parting shot as he retired. The Congress passed the recharter bill, but Jackson vetoed it. This left that institution a lame duck agency.

Jackson soundly defeated Henry Clay in the presidential race and he considered his victory a mandate from the people to destroy the Bank. His first move was to remove the federal government's deposits from Biddle's vaults and distribute the funds to various state and local banks, called by his critics the "pet banks." Biddle responded by tightening up on credit and calling in loans, hoping to embarrass the government and force a withdrawal by Jackson. Jackson stood firm and the result was a financial recession.

When Biddle was forced to relent through pressure from business interests, the economy immediately rebounded. With credit policies relaxed, inflation began to pick up. The government contributed to this expansion by offering millions of acres of western land for sale to settlers at low prices.

In 1836, Jackson ordered a distribution of surplus funds and thus helped to further fuel the inflationary rise in prices. Finally, even Jackson recognized the danger, and tried to slow the spiral by issuing the Specie Circular, which required payment for public land in hard money; no more paper or credit. Depression quickly followed this move.

The business recession lasted well into the 1840's. Our national economy was by this time so tied in with international business and finance that the downturn affected the entire Atlantic community, and was in turn worsened by the global impact. But most Americans blamed everyone in power, including Jackson, and our institutions and business practices. This disillusionment helped to initiate and intensify the reform movement which so occupied this nation in the 19th century's second quarter.

4.10 THE ELECTION OF 1836

Jackson had hand-picked his Democratic successor, Martin Van Buren of New York. The Whigs ran three regional candidates in hopes of upsetting the Jacksonians. The Whig Party had emerged from the ruins of the National Republicans and other groups who opposed Jackson's policies. The name was taken from the British Whig tradition, which simply refers to the "opposition."

4.11   VAN BUREN'S PRESIDENCY

Van Buren, known as Old Kinderhook (O.K.), inherited all the problems and resentments generated by his mentor. He spent most of his term in office dealing with the financial chaos left by the death of the Second Bank. The best he could do was to eventually persuade Congress to establish an Independent Treasury to handle government funds. It began functioning in 1840.

4.12   THE ELECTION OF 1840

4.12.1   *The Candidates*

The Whigs nominated William Henry Harrison, "Old Tippecanoe," Western Indian fighter. Their choice for vice president was John Tyler, a former Democrat from Virginia.

The Democrats put up Van Buren again, but they could not agree on a vice presidential candidate, so they ran no one.

4.12.2   *The Campaign*

This election saw the largest voter turnout to date. The campaign was a dramatic one. The Whigs stressed the depression and the opulent lifestyle of the incumbent in contrast to the simple "log cabin" origins of their candidate.

Harrison won a narrow popular victory, but swept 80% of the electoral vote.

4.12.3   *The Lost Victory*

President Harrison died only a month after the inauguration, having served the shortest term in our presidential history. Tyler assumed the office and immediately reverted to his Democratic origins, thwarting the Whig program. He vetoed most of their attempts at legislation, and most of his cabinet resigned in protest.

4.13 THE MEANING OF JACKSONIAN POLITICS

4.13.1 *The Party System*

The Age of Jackson was the beginning of the modern two-party system. Popular politics, based on emotional appeal, became the accepted style. The practice of meeting in mass conventions to nominate national candidates for office was established during these Jackson years.

4.13.2 *The Strong Executive*

Jackson, more than any president before him, used his office to dominate his party and the government to such an extent that he was called "King Andrew" by his critics.

4.13.3 *The Changing Emphasis Towards States' Rights*

Andrew Jackson supported the authority of the states against the national government, but he drew the line at the concept of nullification. He advocated a strong union made up of sovereign states, and that created some dissonance in his political thinking.

The Supreme Court reflected this shift in thinking in its decision on the Charles River Bridge case in 1837, delivered by Jackson's new Chief Justice, Roger Taney. He ruled that a state could abrogate a grant of monopoly if that original grant had ceased to be in the best interests of the community. This was clearly a reversal of the Dartmouth College principal of the sanctity of contracts, if the general welfare was involved.

4.13.4 *Party Philosophies*

The Democrats opposed big government and the requirements of modernization: urbanization and industrialization. Their support came from the working classes, small merchants, and small farmers.

The Whigs promoted government participation in commercial and industrial development, the encouragement of banking and corporations, and a cautious approach to westward expansion. Their support came largely from Northern business and manufacturing interests, and from large Southern planters. Calhoun, Clay, and Webster dominated the Whig party during these early decades of the 19th century.

4.14 TOCQUEVILLE'S *DEMOCRACY IN AMERICA*

Alexis de Tocqueville, a French civil servant, traveled to this country in the early 1830's to study the American prison system, which was one of the more innovative systems in the world. His book, *Democracy in America*, published in 1835, was the result of his observations, and it reflected a broad interest in the entire spectrum of the American democratic process and the society in which it had developed. His insightful commentary on the American way of life has proven to be almost prophetic in many respects, and provides the modern reader with an outsider's objective view of what this country was like in the Age of Jackson.

CHAPTER 5

ANTE-BELLUM CULTURE: AN AGE OF REFORM

The American people in 1840 found themselves living in an era of transition and instability. The society was changing and traditional values were being challenged. The responses to this uncertainty were two-fold: a movement toward reform and a rising desire for order and control.

We have a fairly vivid picture of what Americans were like in this period of time, from accounts by hundreds of foreign visitors who came to this country to observe our society-in-the-making. These observers noted a restless population, always on the move, compulsive joiners of associations, committed to progress, hard-working and hard-playing, driven relentlessly by a desire for wealth. They believed in and talked about equality, but the reality was that the system was increasingly creating a class society. Americans seemed to lean toward violence, and mob incidents were common.

5.1 THE REFORM IMPULSE

5.1.1 *Major Sources of Reform*

Romanticism. The belief in the innate goodness of man, thus in his improvability. This movement had its roots in turn-of-the-century Europe, and it emphasized the emotions and feelings over rationality. It appeared as a reaction against the excesses of the Enlightenment which had put strong emphasis on reason, to the exclusion of feelings.

The Desire for Order and Stability. There was a growing need perceived for control over the social order and the forces which were threatening the traditional values.

Both of these major streams of reform activity were centered in the Northeast, especially in New England.

5.2 THE FLOWERING OF LITERATURE

5.2.1 *Northern Writers and Themes*

James Fenimore Cooper. His *Leatherstocking Tales* emphasized the independence of the individual, and also the importance of a stable social order.

Walt Whitman. His *Leaves of Grass* likewise celebrated the importance of individualism.

Henry Wadsworth Longfellow. His epic poems *Evangeline* and *Hiawatha* spoke of the value of tradition, and the impact of the past on the present.

Herman Melville. His classic stories — *Typee*, *Billy Budd*, *Moby Dick* — all lashed out at the popular optimism of his day. He believed in the Puritan doctrine of original sin and his characters spoke of the mystery of life.

Francis Parkman. Historian and nationalist, his *Montcalm and Wolfe* vividly portrayed the struggle for empire between France and Britain. *The Oregon Trail* described the opening frontier of the Rocky Mountains and beyond.

James Russell Lowell. Poet and editor, he wrote the *Bigelow Papers* and the *Commemoration Ode* honoring Civil War casualties of Harvard.

Nathaniel Hawthorne. Writer of romances and tales, he is best remembered for his criticism of Puritan bigotry in *The Scarlet Letter*.

5.2.2 Southern Writers and Themes

Edgar Allan Poe. Author of *The Raven*, *Tamerlane* and many tales of terror and darkness, he explored the world of the spirit and the emotions.

William Gilmore Simms. This South Carolina poet changed from a staunch nationalist to a defender of the slave system and the uniqueness of the Southern way of life.

Augustus Longstreet. A Georgia storyteller, he used vulgar, earthy language and themes to paint the common folk of the South.

5.3 THE FINE ARTS

5.3.1 *Artists and Themes*

The Hudson River School was a group of landscape painters who portrayed the awesomeness of nature in America, the new world. George Catlin painted the American Indian, whom he saw as a vanishing race. John James Audubon painted the wide array of American birds and animals.

5.3.2 *Music and the Theatre*

The theatre was popular, but generally condemned by the church and conservatives as a "vagabond profession." The only original American contribution was the blackface minstrel show.

5.4 THE TRANSCENDENTALISTS

5.4.1 *Major Themes*

This movement had its origins in Concord, Massachusetts. The basic objective of these thinkers was to transcend the bounds of the intellect and to strive for emotional understanding, to attain unity with God, without the help of the institutional church, which they saw as reactionary and stifling to self-expression.

5.4.2 *Major Writers*

Ralph Waldo Emerson, essayist and lecturer, authored "Nature" and "Self-Reliance." Henry David Thoreau, best known for his *Walden*, repudiated the repression of society, and preached civil disobedience to protest unjust laws.

5.5 THE UTOPIANS

5.5.1 *Their Purpose*

The cooperative community was their attempt to improve the life of the common man in the face of increasing impersonal industrialism.

5.5.2 *The Utopian Communities*

Brook Farm, in Massachusetts, was the earliest commune in America, and it was short-lived. Nathaniel Hawthorne was a short-term resident, and his *Blithedale Romance* was drawn from that experience. This work and *The Scarlet Letter* were both condemnations of the life of social isolation.

New Harmony, Indiana was founded by Robert Owen, of the New Lanark experiment in Wales, but it failed after two years. He attacked religion, marriage, and the institution of private property, so he encountered resistance from neighboring communities.

Nashoba was in the environs of Memphis, Tennessee, established by the free-thinking Englishwoman Frances Wright as a communal haven for freed slaves. Needless to say, her community experiment encountered fierce opposition from her slave-holding neighbors and it survived only briefly.

Oneida Community in New York was based on free love and open marriages.

The Shakers were directed by Mother Ann Lee. The communities were socialistic experiments which practiced celibacy, sexual equality and social discipline. The name was given them by onlookers at their community dancing sessions.

Amana Community, in Iowa, was another socialist experiment, with a rigidly ordered society.

5.6 THE MORMONS

5.6.1 *The Origins of the Movement*

Joseph Smith received the "sacred" writings in New York state in 1830, and organized the Church of Jesus Christ of Latter Day Saints. They were not popular with their neighbors, primarily because of their practice of polygamy, and so were forced to move about, first to Missouri, then to Nauvoo, Illinois. There Smith was killed by a mob, and the community was led to the Great Salt Lake by their new leader, Brigham Young, in one of the great epic migrations to the West.

5.6.2 *The Church*

The Mormons were the most successful of the communal experiments. They established a highly organized, centrally controlled system, which provided security and order for the faithful. They held a strong belief in human perfectability, and so were in the mainstream of romantic utopians.

5.7 REMAKING SOCIETY: ORGANIZED REFORM

5.7.1 *Sources of Inspiration*

Transcendentalism, as a branch of European Romanticism, spawned a great deal of interest in remaking society into more humane forms.

Protestant Revivalism was a powerful force for the improvement of society. Evangelist Charles G. Finney, through his "social gospel," offered salvation to all. A strong sectarian spirit split the Protestant movement into many groups, such as the Cumberland Presbyterians. Also evident was a strong anti-Catholic element, which was strengthened by the new waves of immigration from Catholic Ireland and southern Germany after 1830.

5.7.2 Reform Movements

Temperance. The American Society for Promotion of Temperance was organized in 1826. It was strongly supported by Protestants, but just as strongly opposed by the new Catholic immigrants.

Public Schools. The motivations for the free school crusade were mixed. Some wanted to provide opportunity for all children to learn the skills for self-fulfillment and success in a republic. Others wanted to use schools as agencies for social control — to Americanize the new immigrant children as well as to Protestantize the Catholics, and to defuse the growing problems of urbanization. The stated purpose of the public schools was to instill social values: thrift, order, discipline, democracy.

Public apathy and even opposition met the early reformers: Horace Mann, the first secretary of the Massachusetts Board of Education, and Henry Barnard, his counterpart in Connecticut and Rhode Island.

The movement picked up momentum in the 1830's, but was very spotty. Few public schools were available in the West, fewer still for Southern whites, and none at all for Southern blacks.

Higher Education. In 1839, the first state-supported school for women, Troy Female Seminary, was founded in Troy, New York. Oberlin College in Ohio was the nation's first co-educational college. The Perkins School for the Blind in Boston was the first of its kind in the United States.

Asylums for the Mentally Ill. Dorothea Dix led the fight for these institutions, advocating more humane treatment for the mentally incompetent.

Prison Reform. The purpose of the new penitentiaries was not to just punish, but to rehabilitate. The first was built in Auburn, New York, in 1821.

Feminism. The Seneca Falls, New York, meeting in 1848, and its "Declaration of Sentiments and Resolutions," was the beginning of the modern feminist movement. The Grimke sisters, Elizabeth Cady Stanton, and Harriet Beecher Stowe were active in these early days. The movement was linked with that of the abolitionists, but suffered because it was considered to be of secondary importance.

5.7.3 The Abolitionist Movement

The early anti-slavery movement was benign, advocating only the purchase and colonization of slaves. The American Colonization Society was organized in 1817 and established the colony of Liberia in 1830, but by that time the movement had reached a dead end.

In 1831, William Lloyd Garrison started his paper, *The Liberator*, and began to advocate total and immediate emancipation, thus giving new life to the movement. He founded the New England Anti-slavery Society in 1832, and the American Anti-slavery Society in 1833.

Theodore Weld pursued the same goals, but advocated more gradual means.

Frederick Douglass, having escaped from his Maryland owner, became a fiery orator for the movement, and published his own newspaper, the *North Star*.

There were frequent outbursts of anti-abolition violence in the 1830's, against the fanaticism of the radicals. Abolitionist editor Elijah Lovejoy was killed by a mob in Illinois.

The movement split into two wings: Garrison's radical followers, and the moderates who favored "moral suasion" and petitions to Congress.

In 1840, the Liberty Party, the first national anti-slavery party, fielded a presidential candidate on the platform of "free soil," non-expansion of slavery into the new western territories.

The literary crusade continued with Harriet Beecher Stowe's *Uncle Tom's Cabin* being the most influential among the many books which presented the abolitionist message.

5.7.4 *Educating the Public*

This was the golden age of oratory. Speechmaking drew huge and patient crowds, and four-hour-long orations were not uncommon, especially at public events like the Fourth of July celebrations.

Newspapers and magazines multiplied and were available to everyone.

Women more and more became the market for magazines oriented to their interests. Periodicals like *Godey's Ladies Book* reached mass circulation figures.

Colleges sprang up everywhere, the products of religious sectarianism as well as local pride, which produced "booster colleges" in every new community as population moved west. Many of these were poorly funded and managed; many did not survive longer than a few years.

Informal educational "lyceums" became popular, where the public could gather for cultural enrichment.

CHAPTER 6

DIVERGING SOCIETIES — LIFE IN THE NORTH

Although the United States was a political entity, with all of the institutions of government and society shared among the peoples of the various states, there had always been a wide diversity of cultural and economic goals among the various states of the union. As the 19th century progressed, that diversity seemed to grow more pronounced, and the collection of states seemed to polarize more into the two sections we call the North and the South, with the expanding West becoming ever more identified with the North.

6.1 POPULATION GROWTH, 1790 – 1860

The new West was the fastest growing area of the country, with population tending to move along parallels westward. From four million in 1790, population had reached 32 million in 1860 with one-half living in states and territories which did not even exist in Washington's administration.

6.1.1 *Natural Increase*

Birth rates began to drop after 1800, more rapidly in the cities than in the rural areas. Families who had averaged six children in 1800 only had five in 1860. Some of the reasons were economic: children were becoming liabilities rather than assets. The new "cult of domesticity" reflected a shift in family responsibilities. Father was out of the home working, and the burden of child-rearing fell more heavily on mother. Primitive birth control methods were used, and abortion was becoming common enough that several states passed laws restricting it. One result of all this was an aging population with the median age rising from 16 to 20 years.

6.1.2 *Immigration*

The influx of immigrants had slowed during the conflicts with France and England, but the flow increased between 1815 and 1837, when the economic downturn again sharply reduced their numbers. Thus the overall rise in population during these years was due more to incoming foreigners than to natural increase. Most of the newcomers were from Britain, Germany and southern Ireland. The Germans usually fared best, since they brought more money and more skills. Discrimination was common in the job market, primarily directed against the Catholics. "Irish Need Not Apply" signs were common. However, the persistent labor shortage prevented the natives from totally excluding the foreign elements. These newcomers huddled in ethnic neighborhoods in the cities, or those who could moved on West to try their hand at farming.

6.2   GROWTH OF THE CITIES

In 1790 5% of the U.S. population lived in cities of 2,500

SOURCES OF IMMIGRATION, 1820 – 1840

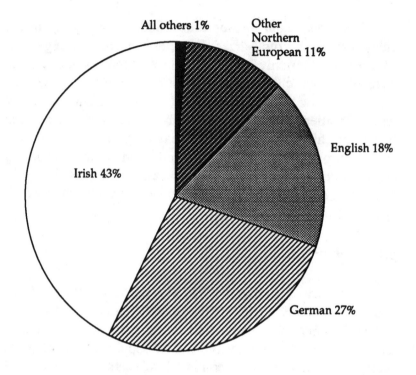

All others 1%

Other
Northern
European 11%

English 18%

Irish 43%

German 27%

or more. By 1860, that figure had risen to 25%. This rapid urbanization created an array of problems.

6.2.1 *Problems of Urbanization*

The rapid growth in urban areas was not matched by the growth of services. Clean water, trash removal, housing and public transportation all lagged behind, and the wealthy got them first. Bad water and poor sanitation produced poor health, and epidemics of typhoid fever, typhus and cholera were common. Police and fire protection were usually inadequate and the development of professional forces was resisted because of the cost and the potential for political patronage and corruption.

TOTAL IMMIGRATION, 1820 – 1840

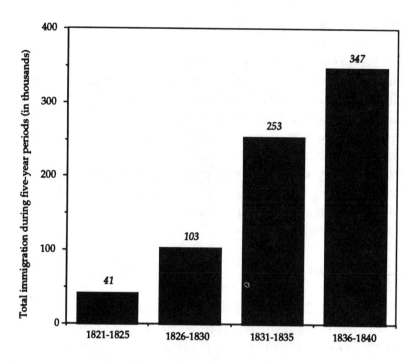

6.2.2   Social Unrest

Rapid growth helped to produce a wave of violence in the cities. In New York City in 1834, the Democrats fought the Whigs with such vigor that the state militia had to be called in. New York and Philadelphia witnessed race riots in the mid-1830's, and a New York mob sacked a Catholic convent in 1834. In the 1830's, 115 major incidents of mob violence were recorded. Street crime was common in all the major cities.

6.3 THE ROLE OF MINORITIES

6.3.1 *Women*

Women were treated as minors before the law. In most states the woman's property became her husband's with marriage. Political activity was limited to the formation of associations in support of various pious causes, such as abolition, and religious and benevolent activity. Professional employment was largely limited to schoolteaching; that occupation became dominated by women. The women's rights movement focused on social and legal discrimination, and women like Lucretia Mott and Sojourner Truth became well-known figures on the speakers' circuit.

6.3.2 *Blacks*

By 1850, 200,000 free blacks lived in the North and West. Their lives were restricted everywhere by prejudice, and "Jim Crow" laws separated the races. Black citizens organized separate churches and fraternal orders. The African Methodist Episcopal Church, for example, had been organized in 1794 in Philadelphia, and flourished in the major Northern cities. Black Masonic and Odd Fellows lodges were likewise established. The economic security of the free blacks was constantly threatened by the newly-arrived immigrants, who were willing to work at the least desirable jobs for less wages. Racial violence was a daily threat.

6.4 THE GROWTH OF INDUSTRY

By 1850, the value of industrial output had surpassed that of agricultural production. The Northeastern states led the way in this movement. Over one-half of the manufacturing establishments were located there, and most of the larger enterprises. Seventy percent of the workers who were employed in manufacturing lived in New England and the middle states, and the Northeast produced more than two-thirds of the manufactured goods.

6.4.1 Inventions and Technology

The level of technology used in American manufacturing already exceeded that of European industry. Eli Whitney's applications of interchangeable parts were being introduced into a wide variety of manufacturing processes. Coal was replacing water as the major source of industrial power. Machine tools were reaching a high level of sophistication. Much of this progress was due to the contributions of America's inventors. Between 1830 and 1850 the number of patents issued for industrial inventions almost doubled. Charles Goodyear's process of vulcanizing rubber was put to 500 different uses and formed the basis for an entire new industry. Elias Howe's sewing machine was to revolutionize the clothing industry. The mass production of iron, with its new techniques and uses, created a new array of businesses, of which the new railroad industry was the largest consumer. Samuel B. Morse's new electric telegraph was first used in 1840 to transmit business news and information.

6.4.2 The Rise of Unions

The growth of the factory system was accompanied by the growth of the corporate form of business ownership, which in turn further separated the owners from the workers. One result was the organization of worker groups to fight for benefits, an early example of which was the 10-hour day. In 1835, Boston construction craftsmen struck for seven months to win a 10-hour work day, and Paterson, New Jersey textile workers became the first factory workers to strike for shorter hours. The federal government's introduction of the 10-hour day for federal projects, in 1840, helped to speed the acceptance of this goal. The influx of immigrants who were willing to work for low wages helped to spur the drive for unions, and in turn their numbers helped to weaken the bargaining position of union members.

6.5   THE REVOLUTION IN AGRICULTURE

Farm and industry reinforced each other and developed simultaneously. As more urban workers became dependent on food grown by others, the potential profits of farming increased. Many of the technological developments and inventions were applied to farm machinery, which in turn enabled farmers to produce more food more cheaply for the urban workers. As in industry, specialization and mechanization became the rule in agriculture, particularly on the newly opening western prairies of Illinois, Iowa and Kansas.

6.5.1   *Inventions and Technology*

Large-scale farming on the prairies spurred critical inventions. McCormick's mechanical reaper, patented in 1834, enabled a crew of six men to harvest in one day as much wheat as 15 men could using older methods. John Deere's steel plow, patented in 1837, provided a more durable tool to break the heavy prairie sod. Jerome Case's threshing machine multiplied the bushels of grain that could be separated from the stalk in a day's time.

6.5.2   *The New Market Economy*

These developments not only made large-scale production

possible, they also shifted the major emphasis from corn to small grain production, and made farming for the international market feasible, which in turn made the western farmer dependent on economic forces over which he had no control. This dependence produced the rising demand for government provision of free land and the agricultural colleges which later were provided by the Homestead and Morrill bills during the Civil War.

In the East, the trend was toward truck farming for the nearby burgeoning urban areas, and the production of milk, fruits and berries. Here, as in the West, there was much interest in innovative practices which could increase production efficiency and profits.

6.6   THE REVOLUTION IN COMMERCE

Before the coming of the railroad, coastal sailing ships practically monopolized domestic trade. The canal construction boom of the 1830's had taken commercial traffic from the river systems, but by 1840 the railroad had begun to emerge as the carrier of the future. Pennsylvania and New York State contained most of the 3,328 miles of track, but the rail system was rapidly expanding across the northern tier of states, tying the industrializing East to the expanding, agricultural West.

6.7   EVERYDAY LIFE IN THE NORTH

Between 1800 and 1860 output of goods and services increased twelve-fold and the purchasing power of the average worker doubled. The household labor system was breaking down, and the number of wage-earners exceeded for the first time the numbers of independent, self-employed Americans. Even so, everyday living was still quite primitive. Most people bathed only infrequently, washed clothes and dishes even less. Housing was primitive for most, consisting of one- or two-room cabins, heated by open fireplaces, with water carried in from springs or public faucets. For the working man, rural or urban, life was hard.

CHAPTER 7

DIVERGING SOCIETIES — LIFE IN THE SOUTH

The Southern states experienced dramatic growth in the second quarter of the 19th century. The economy grew more productive and more prosperous, but still the section called the South was basically agrarian, with few important cities and scattered industry. The plantation system, with its cash crop production driven by the use of slave labor, remained the dominant institution. In the words of one historian, "The South *grew*, but it did not develop." And so the South grew more and more unlike the North, and it became more and more defensive of its distinctive way of life.

7.1   THE COTTON KINGDOM

The most important economic phenomenon of the early decades of the 19th century was the shift in population and production from the old "upper South" of Virginia and the Carolinas to the "lower South" of the newly opened Gulf States of Alabama, Mississippi, and Louisiana. This shift was the direct result of the increasing importance of cotton. In the older Atlantic states, tobacco retained its importance, but had shifted westward to the Piedmont, and was replaced in the east by food grains. The southern Atlantic coast continued to produce rice and southern Louisiana and east Texas retained their emphasis on sugar cane. But the rich black soil of the new Gulf states proved ideal for the production of short-staple cotton, especially after the invention of the "gin", and cotton became the center of the Southern economy. Nearly three million bales were being produced annually by 1850.

By 1860, cotton was to account for two-thirds of the value of U.S. exports. In the words of a Southern legislator of that era, "Cotton is King!"

7.2 CLASSES IN THE SOUTH

Although the large plantation with its white-columned mansion and its aristocratic owners is frequently seen as typical of Southern life, the truth is quite different.

7.2.1 *The Planter Class*

Owners of large farms who also owned 50 or more slaves actually formed a small minority of the Southern population. Three-fourths of Southern whites owned no slaves at all, almost half of slave-owning families owned fewer than six, and 12 percent owned 20 or more. But this minority of large slave-owners exercised political and economic power far beyond what their numbers would indicate. They became a class to which all others paid deference, and they dominated the political and social life of their region.

WHITE SOCIAL STRUCTURE IN THE SOUTH, 1860

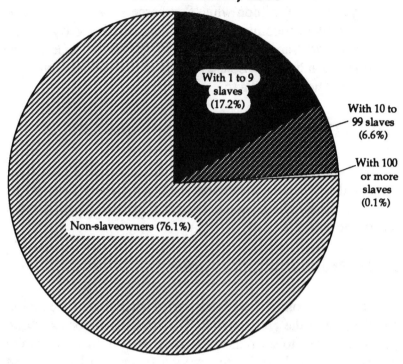

With 1 to 9 slaves (17.2%)

With 10 to 99 slaves (6.6%)

With 100 or more slaves (0.1%)

Non-slaveowners (76.1%)

7.2.2 *The Yeoman Farmers*

The largest group of Southern whites were the independent small farmers who worked their land with their family, sometimes side-by-side with one or two slaves, to produce their own food, with sometimes enough surplus to sell for a little extra cash. These simple folk predominated in the upland South and constituted a sizeable element even in the lower cotton-producing states. Their major crop was corn, and indeed the South's corn crop was more valuable than its cotton, but the corn was used at home for dinner tables and for animal feed, and so ranked behind cotton as an item of export. These people were generally poorer than their Northern counterparts.

7.2.3 *The Poor Whites*

Perhaps a half-million white Southerners lived on the edge of the agrarian economy, in varying degrees of poverty. These "crackers," or "sandhillers," occupied the barren soils of the red hills or sandy bottoms, and they lived in squalor worse than the slaves. They formed a true underclass.

7.3   THE INSTITUTION OF SLAVERY

As the necessary concomitant of this expanding plantation system, the "Peculiar Institution" of black slavery fastened itself upon the Southern people, even as it isolated them from the rest of the world.

7.3.1 *Slavery as a Labor System*

The utilization of slave labor varied according to the region and the size of the growing unit. The large plantations growing cotton, sugar or tobacco used the gang system, in which white overseers directed black drivers, who supervised large groups of workers in the fields, all performing the same operation. In the culture of rice, and on the smaller farms, slaves were assigned specific tasks, and when those tasks were finished, the worker had the remainder of the day to himself.

House servants usually were considered the most favored since they were spared the hardest physical labor and enjoyed the most intimate relationship with the owner's family. This could be considered a drawback, since they were frequently deprived of the social communion of the other slaves, enjoyed less privacy, and were more likely to suffer the direct wrath of a dissatisfied mistress.

GROWTH OF SLAVE LABOR, 1800 – 1860

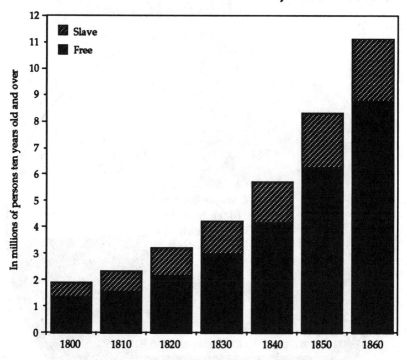

Historians still debate whether the Southern plantation slaves fared better or worse then the Northern wage laborers. Certainly their lot was better than their counterparts in South America and the Caribbean.

7.3.2 *Urban Slavery in the Southern City*

A sizeable number of black slaves worked in the towns, serving as factory hands, domestics, artisans, and construction workers. They lived fairly independent lives and indeed a good number purchased their freedom with their savings, or quietly crossed the color line and disappeared into the general population. As the 19th century progressed, these people were increasingly seen as a bad model and a threat to the institution, and so urban slavery practically disappeared.

BLACK SOCIAL STRUCTURE IN
THE OLD SOUTH, 1860

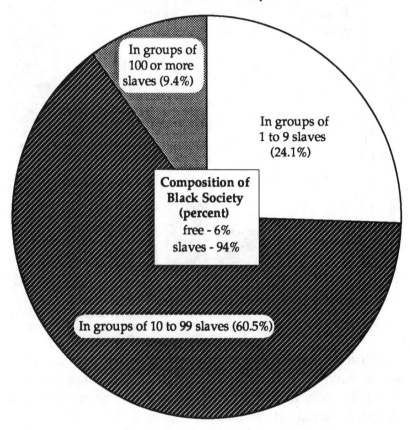

In groups of
100 or more
slaves (9.4%)

In groups of
1 to 9 slaves
(24.1%)

Composition of
Black Society
(percent)
free - 6%
slaves - 94%

In groups of 10 to 99 slaves (60.5%)

7.3.3 *The Slave Trade*

The most significant demographic shift in these decades
was the movement of blacks from the Old South to the new
Southwest. Traders shipped servants by the thousands to the
newly opened cotton lands of the gulf states. A prime field
hand fetched an average price of $800, as high as $1500 in
peak years. Families were frequently split apart by this miser-
able traffic. Planters freely engaged in this trade, but assigned
very low status to the traders who carried it out.

Although the importation of slaves from abroad had been outlawed by Congress since 1808, they continued to be smuggled in until the 1850's. The import ban kept the price up and encouraged the continuation of the internal trade.

7.3.4 Slaves' Reaction to Slavery

Blacks in bondage suffered varying degrees of repression and deprivation. The harsh slave codes were comprehensive in their restrictions on individual freedom, but they were unevenly applied, and so there was considerable variety in the severity of life. The typical slave probably received a rough but adequate diet and enjoyed crude but sufficient housing and clothing.

But the loss of freedom and the injustice of the system produced a variety of responses. Many "soldiered" on the job, and refused to work hard, or they found ways to sabotage the machinery or the crops. There was an underground system of ridicule toward the masters which was nurtured, as reflected in such oral literature as the "Brer Rabbit" tales.

Violent reaction to repression was not uncommon. Gabriel Prosser in Richmond (1800), Denmark Vesey in Charleston (1822), and Nat Turner in coastal Virginia (1831) all plotted or led uprisings of blacks against their white masters. Rumors of such uprisings kept whites in a state of constant apprehension.

The ultimate rebellion was to simply leave, and many tried to run away, some successfully. Especially from the states bordering the North, an ever increasing number of slaves fled to freedom, many with the aid of the "underground railroad" and smugglers such as Harriet Tubman, who led over 300 of her family and friends to freedom after she herself had escaped.

Most of those in bondage, however, were forced to simply adapt, and they did. A rich culture was developed within the confines of the system, and included distinctive patterns of language, music and religion. Kinship ties were probably strengthened in the face of the onslaughts of sale and separation of family members. In the face of incredible odds, the slaves developed a distinctive network of tradition and interdependence, and they survived.

7.4   COMMERCE AND INDUSTRY

The lack of manufacturing and business development has frequently been blamed for the South's losing its bid for independence in 1861 – 1865. Actually the South was highly industrialized for its day, and compared favorably with most European nations in the development of manufacturing capacity. Obviously, it trailed far behind its neighbors to the North, so much so that when war erupted in 1861, the Northern states owned 81 percent of the factory capacity in the United States.

7.4.1   *Manufacturing*

The southern states saw considerable development in the 1820's and 1830's in textiles and iron production and in flour milling. Richmond's Tredegar Iron Works compared favorably with the best in the North. Montgomery Bell's forges in Tennessee produced a good proportion of the ironware used in the upper South. Even so, most of the goods manufactured in these plants were for plantation consumption rather than for export, and they never exceeded two percent of the value of the cotton crop.

7.4.2 Commercial Activity

The businessmen of the South worked primarily with the needs and products of the plantation and the factors of New Orleans and Charleston had to serve as bankers and insurance brokers as well as the agents for the planters. An organized network of commerce never developed in the South, even though the planters themselves must be recognized as businessmen, since they operated large, complex staple-producing units.

7.4.3 Voices for Change

There were those who saw their native South sinking ever more into the position of dependency upon Northern bankers and businessmen, and they cried out for reform. James B.D. DeBow's *Review* advocated commercial development and agricultural diversification, but his cries largely fell on deaf ears.

Why were Southerners so wedded to the plantation system, in the face of much evidence that it was retarding development? Certainly one reason is that cotton was profitable. Over the long run, capital return on plantation agriculture was at least as good as on Northern industrial capital. Even though skilled slaves abounded and could have manned factories, they were more profitable in the field.

Since most of the planter's capital was tied up in land and slaves, there was little left to invest in commerce or manufacturing. Most important, perhaps, was the value system of the Southern people, who put great store in traditional rural ideals: chivalry, leisure, genteel elegance. Even the yeoman farmer held these values, and hoped some day to attain to the position the planters held.

7.5 LIFE IN THE SOUTHERN STATES

7.5.1 *The Role of Women*

The position of the Southern woman was similar in many ways to her Northern counterpart, but also very different. They had fewer opportunities for anything but home life. The middle-class wife was heavily involved in the operation of the farm, and served as supervisor and nurse for the servants as well as manager of the household, while the upper class women served merely as ornaments. Education was rare, and centered on the "domestic arts." High birth and death rates took their toll on childbearing women, and many men outlived several wives. The half-breed slave children were constant reminders of the planters' dalliances and produced constant tension and frustration among plantation wives.

7.5.2 *Education*

Schooling beyond literacy training was available only to the sons of the well-to-do. Academics and colleges abounded, but not for the working classes. And what public schools there were, were usually inferior and ill-supported. By 1860, one-half of all the illiterates in the United States lived in the South.

7.5.3 *Daily Life in the South*

The accounts of travelers in the Southern states provide us with vivid pictures of living conditions on the average homestead. Housing was primitive, one or two-room cabins being the rule. Corn, sweet potatoes, and pork formed the staples of the Southern diet and health problems reflected the resulting vitamin deficiencies. Rickets and pellagra were common ailments.

Although the prevalence of violence has probably been overstated, it certainly existed and the duel remained an accepted avenue for settling differences well into the 19th century.

7.6 SOUTHERN RESPONSE TO THE ANTI-SLAVERY MOVEMENT

As the crusade for abolition intensified in the North, the South assumed an ever more defensive position. Biblical texts were used to justify the enslavement of an "inferior race." Scientific arguments were advanced to prove the inherent inferiority of the black African. Southern postal authorities refused to deliver any mail that contained information antagonistic to the slave system. Any kind of dissent was brutally suppressed, and the South became more and more a closed society. Literature and scholarship shriveled, and creative writers like Edgar Allan Poe and William Gilmore Simms became the rare exception.

The last serious Southern debate over the institution of slavery took place in the Virginia legislature in 1832, in the aftermath of Nat Turner's revolt. That discussion squelched any move toward emancipation. In 1836 Southern members of the U.S. House of Representatives pushed through the infamous "gag rule," which forbade any discussion on the question of slavery on the floor of the House. That rule remained in effect until 1844.

The most elaborate product of this ferment was John C. Calhoun's theory of the "concurrent majority," in which a dual presidency would insure a South independent of Northern dominance, and would forever keep majority rule at bay.

Beginning in 1837, regular conventions were held across

the South to discuss ways to escape Northern economic and political hegemony.

As the decade of the 1840's opened, the two sections were becoming more and more estranged, and the channels of compromise were becoming more and more poisoned by the emotional responses to black slavery. The development which contributed most to keeping the sore festering was westward expansion.

CHAPTER 8

MANIFEST DESTINY AND WESTWARD EXPANSION

Although the term "Manifest Destiny" was not actually coined until 1844, the belief that the American nation was destined to eventually expand all the way to the Pacific Ocean, and to possibly embrace Canada to the North, and Mexico to the South, had been voiced for years by many who believed that American liberty and ideals should be shared with everyone possible, by force if necessary. The rising sense of nationalism which followed the War of 1812 was fed by the rapidly expanding population, the reform impulse of the 1830's, and the desire to acquire new markets and resources for the burgeoning economy of "Young America."

8.1 LOUISIANA AND THE FAR WEST FUR TRADE

The Lewis and Clark expedition had scarcely filed its reports before a variety of adventurous entrepreneurs began to penetrate the newly acquired territory, and the lands beyond. "Mountain men" like Jim Bridges trapped the Rocky Mountain streams and the headwaters of the Missouri River system for the greatly prized beaver pelts, while explorers like Jedediah Smith mapped the vast territory which stretched from the Rockies to the Sierra Nevada range and on into California. John Jacob Astor established a fur post at the mouth of the Columbia River which he named Astoria, and challenged the British claim to the northwest. Though he was forced to sell out his establishment to the British, he lobbied Congress to pass trade restrictions against British furs, and eventually became the first American millionaire from the profits of the American Fur Company. The growing trade with the Orient in furs and other specialty goods was sharpening the desire of many businessmen for American ports on the Pacific coast.

8.2   THE OREGON COUNTRY

The Adams-Onis Treaty of 1819 had set the northern boundary of Spanish possessions near the present northern border of California. The territory north of that line and west of the vague boundaries of the Louisiana Territory had been claimed over the years by Spain, England, Russia, France, and the United States. By the 1820's, all these claims had been yielded to Britain and the United States. The Hudson's Bay Company had established a fur trading station at Fort Vancouver, and claimed control south to the Columbia. The United States claimed all the way north to the 54°40' parallel. Unable to settle the dispute, they had agreed on a joint occupation of the disputed land.

In the 1830's American missionaries followed the traders and trappers to the Oregon country, and began to publicize the richness and beauty of the land, sending back official reports on their work, which were published in the new inexpensive "penny press" papers. Everyone read these reports, and the result was the "Oregon Fever" of the 1840's, as thousands of settlers trekked across the Great Plains and the Rocky Mountains to settle the new Shangri-La.

8.3   THE TEXAS QUESTION: 1836 – 1845

Texas had been a state in the Republic of Mexico since 1822, following the Mexican revolution against Spanish control. The United States had offered to buy the territory at the time, since it had renounced its claim to the area in the Adams-Onis agreement of 1819. The new Mexican government indignantly refused to sell, but immediately began to invite immigration from the north by offering land grants to Stephen Austin and other Americans. They needed to increase the population of the area and to produce revenue for the infant government. The Americans responded in great numbers, and by 1835 approximately 35,000 "gringos" were homesteading on Texas land.

The Mexican officials saw their power base eroding as the foreigners flooded in, and so they moved to tighten control, through restrictions on new immigration, and through tax increases. The Texans responded in 1836 by proclaiming independence and establishing a new republic. The ensuing war was short-lived. The Mexican dictator, Santa Anna, advanced north and annihilated the Texan garrisons at the Alamo and at Goliad. On April 23, 1836, Sam Houston defeated him at San Jacinto, and the Mexicans were forced to let Texas go its way.

Houston immediately asked the American government for recognition and annexation, but President Andrew Jackson feared the revival of the slavery issue since the new state would come in on the slave-holding side of the political balance, and he also feared war with Mexico, so he did nothing. When Van

THE TEXAS REVOLUTION

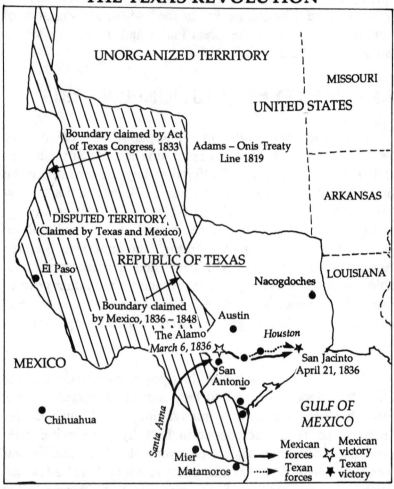

UNORGANIZED TERRITORY

MISSOURI

UNITED STATES

Boundary claimed by Act
of Texas Congress, 1833

Adams – Onis Treaty
Line 1819

ARKANSAS

DISPUTED TERRITORY
(Claimed by Texas and Mexico)

El Paso

REPUBLIC OF TEXAS

LOUISIANA

Nacogdoches

Boundary claimed
by Mexico, 1836 – 1848

Austin

The Alamo
March 6, 1836

Houston

MEXICO

San
Antonio

San Jacinto
April 21, 1836

Chihuahua

Santa Anna

GULF OF
MEXICO

Mier

Matamoros

Mexican
forces

Mexican
victory

Texan
forces

Texan
victory

Buren followed suit, the new republic sought foreign recognition and support, which the European nations eagerly provided, hoping thereby to create a counterbalance to rising American power and influence in the Southwest. France and England both quickly concluded trade agreements with the Texans.

8.4   NEW MEXICO AND CALIFORNIA

The district of New Mexico had, like Texas, encouraged American immigration, and for the same reasons. Soon that state was more American than Mexican. The Santa Fe Trail — from Independence, Missouri, to the town of Santa Fe — created a prosperous trade in mules, gold and silver, and furs which moved north in exchange for manufactured goods which went south. American settlements sprung up all along the route.

Though the Mexican officials in California had not encouraged it, American immigration nevertheless had been substantial. First traders and whaling crews, then merchants, arrived to set up stores and developed a brisk trade. As the decade of the 1830's passed, the number of newcomers increased. Since the Missouri Compromise had established the northern limits for slavery at the 36°30' parallel, most of this Mexican territory lay in the potential slave-holding domain, and many of the settlers had carried their bondsmen with them.

8.5   THE DISPUTE WITH CANADA

Though the issue of slavery was not involved in the northern territory, expansionists were also casting covetous glances toward their Canadian neighbors. The boundary line between Maine and Canada had been disputed ever since the Treaty of Paris in 1783, but the sparse population produced few incidents. A local rebellion among Canadian dissidents in 1837 brought support from neighboring New Yorkers, and the Canadian loyalists had retaliated by crossing the border and burning the American ship *Caroline* and killing an American citizen on New York territory.

In 1839, the Canadians began building a road into the forest on the Maine border, across land claimed by that state. The ensuing Aroostook War, though without serious casualties, heightened the nationalistic feelings in New England, and produced cries to invade and seize Canadian territory. This recurring tension was finally settled by the Webster-Ashburton Agreement of 1842, which established the boundary line where it remains to this day.

8.6 MANIFEST DESTINY AND SECTIONAL STRESS

The question of expansion was universally discussed. Although the strongest sentiment was found in the North and West, the South had its own ambitions, and they usually involved the extension of their "peculiar institution."

The Democrats generally favored the use of force, if necessary, to extend American borders. The Whigs favored more peaceful means, through diplomacy. Some Whigs, like Henry Clay, feared expansion under any circumstances, because of its potential for aggravating the slavery issue.

Clay was closest to the truth. As the decade of the 1840's opened, the questions of Texas, California and the New Mexican territory were increasingly prominent, and the sectional tension which they produced was destined to light the fires of civil war.

Available at your local bookstore or order directly from us by sending in coupon below.

Available at your local bookstore or order directly from us by sending in coupon below.

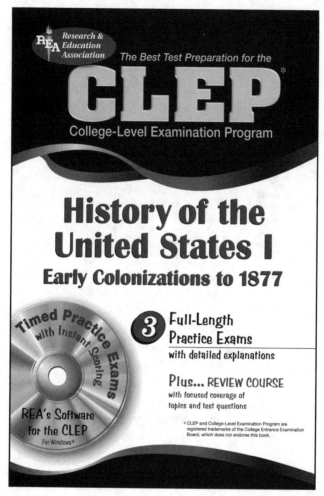

Available at your local bookstore or order directly from us by sending in coupon below.

Available at your local bookstore or order directly from us by sending in coupon below.

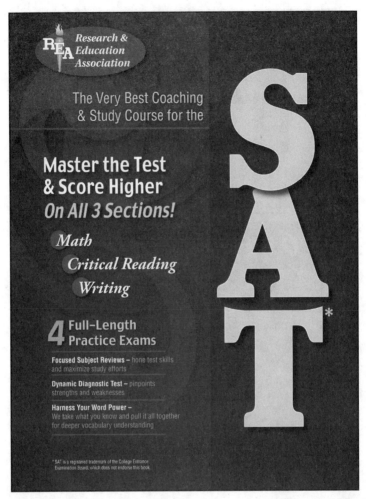

REA'S

PROBLEM SOLVERS®

PROBLEM SOLVERS

Physics

The Perfect Resource for:
- *any class*
- *any exam*
- *any problem*

A Reference for Life

The PROBLEM SOLVERS® are comprehensive supplemental textbooks designed to save time in finding solutions to problems. Each PROBLEM SOLVER® is the first of its kind ever produced in its field. It is the product of a massive effort to illustrate almost any imaginable problem in exceptional depth, detail, and clarity. Each problem is worked out in detail with a step-by-step solution, and the problems are arranged in order of complexity from elementary to advanced. Each book is fully indexed for locating problems rapidly.

Accounting

Advanced Calculus

Algebra & Trigonometry

Automatic Control Systems/Robotics

Business, Accounting & Finance

Calculus

Chemistry

Differential Equations

Electrical Machines

Electric Circuits

Electromagnetics

Electronics

Finite & Discrete Math

Fluid Mechanics/Dynamics

Genetics

Geometry

Linear Algebra

Mechanics

Numerical Analysis

Operations Research

Organic Chemistry

Physics

Pre-Calculus

Probability

Psychology

Statistics

Technical Design Graphics

Thermodynamics

Topology

If you would like more information about any of these books,
complete the coupon below and return it to us or visit your local bookstore.

Research & Education Association
61 Ethel Road W., Piscataway, NJ 08854
Phone: (732) 819-8880   **website: www.rea.com**

Please send me more information about your Problem Solver® books.

Name _____

Address _____

City _____ State _____ Zip _____

MAXnotes®

REA's Literature Study Guides

MAXnotes® are student-friendly. They offer a fresh look at masterpieces of literature, presented in a lively and interesting fashion. **MAXnotes®** offer the essentials of what you should know about the work, including outlines, explanations and discussions of the plot, character lists, analyses, and historical context. **MAXnotes®** are designed to help you think independently about literary works by raising various issues and thought-provoking ideas and questions. Written by literary experts who currently teach the subject, **MAXnotes®** enhance your understanding and enjoyment of the work.

Available **MAXnotes®** include the following:

Absalom, Absalom!
The Aeneid of Virgil
Animal Farm
Antony and Cleopatra
As I Lay Dying
As You Like It
The Autobiography of
      Malcolm X
The Awakening
Beloved
Beowulf
Billy Budd
The Bluest Eye, A Novel
Brave New World
The Canterbury Tales
The Catcher in the Rye
The Color Purple
The Crucible
Death in Venice
Death of a Salesman
Dickens Dictionary
The Divine Comedy I: Inferno
Dubliners
The Edible Woman
Emma
Euripides' Medea & Electra
Frankenstein
Gone with the Wind
The Grapes of Wrath
Great Expectations
The Great Gatsby
Gulliver's Travels
Handmaid's Tale
Hamlet
Hard Times

Heart of Darkness
Henry IV, Part I
Henry V
The House on Mango Street
I Know Why the Caged
      Bird Sings
The Iliad
Invisible Man
Jane Eyre
Jazz
The Joy Luck Club
Jude the Obscure
Julius Caesar
King Lear
Leaves of Grass
Les Misérables
Lord of the Flies
Macbeth
The Merchant of Venice
Metamorphoses of Ovid
Metamorphosis
Middlemarch
A Midsummer Night's Dream
Moll Flanders
Mrs. Dalloway
Much Ado About Nothing
Mules and Men
My Antonia
Native Son
1984
The Odyssey
Oedipus Trilogy
Of Mice and Men
On the Road
Othello

Paradise
Paradise Lost
A Passage to India
Plato's Republic
Portrait of a Lady
A Portrait of the Artist
      as a Young Man
Pride and Prejudice
A Raisin in the Sun
Richard II
Romeo and Juliet
The Scarlet Letter
Sir Gawain and the
      Green Knight
Slaughterhouse-Five
Song of Solomon
The Sound and the Fury
The Stranger
Sula
The Sun Also Rises
A Tale of Two Cities
The Taming of the Shrew
Tar Baby
The Tempest
Tess of the D'Urbervilles
Their Eyes Were Watching
God
Things Fall Apart
To Kill a Mockingbird
To the Lighthouse
Twelfth Night
Uncle Tom's Cabin
Waiting for Godot
Guide to Literary Terms

If you would like more information about any of these books,
complete the coupon below and return it to us or visit your local bookstore.

Research & Education Association
61 Ethel Road W., Piscataway, NJ 08854
Phone: (732) 819-8880   **website: www.rea.com**

Please send me more information about **MAXnotes®**.

Name _____

Address _____

City _____ State _____ Zip _____